# EYES WIDE OPEN

## THE TRANSFORMED ME

### TESHA HALL

EYES WIDE OPEN
*The Transformed Me*

Tesha Hall
dkhall07@icloud.com

ISBN 978-1-949826-55-5

Printed in the USA.
All rights reserved

Published by: EAGLES GLOBAL BOOKS | Frisco, Texas
In conjunction with the 2022 Eagles Authors Course
**Cover & interior designed by DestinedToPublish.com**

# ACKNOWLEDGMENTS

This book is dedicated to my parents, the late Mr. and Mrs. Gregory and Patricia Williams. I could never have made it to become the great woman I am today without their love and correction. My parents always told me to see beyond what I can see and to know that God can make all my impossible, possible. Shout-out to the most amazing husband, Darrel Hall, who has loved me beyond me. I thank you for living out the words "what God put together, let no man separate." To my two beautiful children, Gregory and Taliya, thank y'all for supporting me and always placing a smile on my face. Thank you for being the best *you* that you could possibly be. To my brothers who have walked this journey with me, Gregory Jr., Tyrie, and Preston, we have been through the hardest part of our lives, and guess what, we did it together.

Let's continue to move forward like our parents would want us to. Sherell, thank you for our crazy phone calls and how you are always there for me, I never had a sister, but you are an amazing sister-in-law. To Nicole, thank you for being their thru out one of the toughest times of my life. To my cousins, thank you! Your love for me has never gone unnoticed. Thank you to all of my family, who have always been my biggest supporters.

I thank Destined to Publish for encouraging me to step aside and allow God to have His way. There are many special people in my life who I would like to give a shout-out to! You know who you are. Apostle Camlyn Leander and Wanda Finley, thank you for taking this journey with me. Your words of encouragement and your support were amazing. To Luveria Morris thank you for being an amazing prayer partner and friend. I thank God for this journey called life, because without Him, I would not have made it. I would like to give a shout-out to Jared Merlin, who never allowed me to stay comfortable in one position but encouraged me to be comfortable with being uncomfortable and stretching Me to reach my goals. To my U-Haul work family, I thank you for pushing me to be the best leader I could be. You are an awesome group of people. Keep pushing yourself toward your goals and your dreams – I declare and decree they shall all come to pass. Last but not least, thank you to my New Beginnings Church Family, especially our leader,

# Acknowledgments

Apostle Tami Christian thank you for all your love, support and correction. Thank you for always following the direction of God. Remember that what you do for Christ shall last. Love you all!

# FOREWORD

Knowing whose you are reveals who you are. Your identity, which is in Jesus Christ, allows you to be confident, bold, and focused, and to walk alone knowing that God is with you and He is enough. Identity confusion occurs when you change who you are to become the person everyone will like. Success in this life is having a relationship with your Creator, heavenly Father, submitting to His will for your life, and fulfilling your God-given purpose. Success is returning to Father emptied after living a life poured out.

Through her life journey, Tesha Hall shows us how we can be delivered from people-pleasing and being taken advantage of by others, and delivered into becoming who God created us to be by diligently seeking God, listening for and to His voice, and obeying Him. This book, *Eyes Wide Open*, will help to propel you into your Prophetic Destiny. If you listen intently and follow the steps diligently, you will find yourself light-years ahead and beyond any self-imposed or people-imposed limitations. The BEST version of you is on the other side of this door. Open it and step in.

Apostle Camlyn Leander

# CONTENTS

# INTRODUCTION

Come with me as I share with you how not only did finding my kingdom identity and my divine purpose in God propel me to arise in the kingdom of God, but I was able to apply it to my everyday life, which helped me to move from walking by sight to walking by faith. This process was not an easy one, but it was necessary. This book will remind you that many have walked in the same path you are walking and made it to the end of the path that was set before them. Many have failed, many wanted to quit, but remember that what God has for you is only for you. Stepping out into the unknown is scary, but God will be a lamp unto your path. This book will encourage you to grab hold and embrace the process of change.

I want to help you to understand the importance of finding your kingdom identity, and to understand that until you recognize whose you are, you will never recognize who you are. You were chosen to be part of a royal priesthood, set apart for the works of the kingdom. God loved you so much that even though you didn't choose God, He still chose you.

You will leave this book knowing that identity is what you were created to be and not something that you chose to do! Identity is an action; it takes effort and commitment. You will realize that even though we all have the same DNA from God, we have different identities: who you were made to be could not be carbon copied. Identity is the condition of being oneself, and not another. Our true identity is defined not by our past actions but by the Savior's. Jesus purchased our lives with His blood and brought us into relationship with God the Father, who adopted us as beloved children.

This book will do just that: remind you that you have every reason to hold your head high, stand firm, and courageously proclaim who God has called you to be in the earth realm. I pray through this book that you will align yourself with the will that God has for your life, placing all fleshly desire to the side. I also pray that you will understand that the only way to be truly happy is to live in the fullness of God. There is a nation of people that are called to you, but their purpose and destiny is being delayed because you are still searching for your purpose.

The world is waiting for His sons to arise and take their place. This journey called life is much more than being born to die: it is what you do to be effective in a world of lost souls. Many mistakenly miss their call by God because we consume ourselves with what we believe our call is instead of searching for truth. We stay in a place of comfort because it is a safe place. God is calling for you to arise and take your rightful place in His kingdom. A complete "Yes" is all He needs! It is time to Think Bigger Than That and Believe BY Faith, and the results will be Overflow, Overflow, Overflow! Say to yourself, "Mountain, you no longer stand in my way, for my God said so!" Don't you let nobody turn you around – you got to keep on walking on the path that God set before you. Know that we serve a limitless God and nothing about your journey has caught Him by surprise. You can do all things through Christ who gives you strength.

Eyes Wide Open

# CHAPTER 1

# Who Am I?

Throughout this world, people have asked many questions concerning the purpose of their being. The Bible tells us that before we were formed in our mother's womb, God anointed us, set us apart, and sent us as prophets to the nations. So, if you will allow me, I would like to be the first person to tell you that your purpose is found in your identity. Your identity is what God purposed you to be. There is no one who can do or copycat your kingdom assignment. You are unique; your DNA is yours. And because God has told us that He set us apart and sent us as prophets to the nations, we know that you are a representative of the kingdom of God. The Bible tells us that we were made in the image of Christ, which means that because of who our Savior is, we have limitless victory. The Bible also tells you the thoughts that God has toward you. So, because God says that you are the apple of His eye, because He says in Jeremiah 29:11 that the plans He has for you are to prosper you and not to harm you, and for you to have a bright future, God has set you up to walk in victory moment by moment by the power of the Holy Spirit. God has revealed to you that you are special to Him, and just as a father loves his child and only sees the good in them, God looks at you just like that. He has looked past all your faults and into your heart, not because of any goodness of your own but because He loved you just that much.

The Bible also states that we were created in the image of God. We know so much about God and who He is, especially to you, so why wouldn't you want to adopt His ways? Adopting the ways of God will help you to find your identity. God placed different parts of Himself within you, and this must be embraced to tap into the true you. You were called to be you; can you hear God asking, "How can you be something or someone you don't know"? So, let me help you by sharing with you whose you are. God says you are loved, important, special, kind, unique, pretty, handsome – you are the you He created. God is calling for you to be the best you that you can possibly be! God does not want copycats. What God has for you is only for you. He needs to know He is giving it to the correct person.

I can speak of this process because I had almost given up and thrown in the towel searching for who I thought I was, until God revealed my true identity. This was a long process, but it was worth it. These processes caused me to stop believing in myself for a time. I believed what was said about me and wanted approval from people, so it stopped me from doing what God directed me to do. I wasted so much time because I didn't know the power that I carried and what God was using me for in the earth realm. I was taken advantage of, always wanting to be chosen. People looked past me, and it was what they saw in me that I didn't see in myself. They feared what I was becoming and stuck around me for my boldness, but I allowed myself to be used as I tried to fit in.

I can tell you this part of the process was hurtful and painful. I don't know if I would have been able to make it through if at some point I hadn't prayed and asked God to send me some type of understanding. As time went by, God started to answer me and send some type of confirmation, which then allowed me to start changing the way I thought about myself. I started to see myself differently, and this is when the transformation started. Just know that years passed before I started to understand who I was in God. It took a lot of studying, not only learning the Word of God but understanding the Word and then applying it to my life. Understanding your identity is not something that happens overnight, but if you are determined to seek it, you shall find it.

During this process of not only finding your identity but walking in your purpose, there must be a transformation that takes place. This transformation consists of a change in your state of mind. You must adapt to the mind of Christ and adopt the will that He has for your life. This was one of the hardest steps that I had to take. It is very hard to unlearn everything that you were used to for years. Even though it might not have been correct, I had made it work for me. I was satisfied with being the person I chose to be with no accountability. Then the correction came, and I wasn't ready to receive it – first, because I didn't see the way I was living as wrong, and secondly, because I didn't clearly hear the voice of God, so how would I know what was Him? This was the time in the process when relationship with God meant a lot. How can your mindset change when you were hurt in the past because people didn't like who you were, so you created a person everyone likes, but it wasn't the person God created you to be? I was in a true state of confusion, and only God could answer the questions and feelings I had going on, but my relationship with God was distant. I remember there were many tears during this time, but when I look back now, I wouldn't change anything about what I went through. It was what I needed to get to the place of knowing that I was chosen to be part of a chosen generation, a royal priesthood, and that I was a peculiar person who God called as His prophet.

As I was going through this process, I recall that when I decided to submit my will to God's will, I started to see myself as God saw me. I would say decrees over myself every morning and night. For every negative word that was spoken in my life, I would replace it with three positive words. God allowed me to begin to hear His voice through my voice. It was clear, it was a voice I had heard several times before but couldn't distinguish from the voices of others, but relationship and submission made the difference. The change of mindset was something that I had to constantly work on, reminding myself that I was created in the image of God and allowing myself to know that I'm God's masterpiece even when I didn't see it that way.

You must know that you were handpicked and chosen by the Father Himself. God sees you as the apple of His eye and His perfect love. That is why He promised you a bright future. God thinks so much about you that He revealed to the world that you are part of a royal priesthood, a chosen generation. You are loved by the Most High God, and because of that, you are a light in a dark place. This is the first part of what your identity is. When you see yourself as God sees you, there will be a time when you look in the mirror and realize that you share the DNA of a God who is mighty, your undefeated champion, your banner of love, the only provider, a holy King, the light of the world, a strong tower, the one who created heaven and earth, Love, the one who sent His Son to die on the cross so that we can have everlasting life. When you are seen by the Father, He looks past every one of your faults and sees directly to your heart. He sees you like you see your own children, beautiful and faultless.

Understanding how you are seen by the Father is the only way to embrace your identity. You will develop a boldness and a passion for your willingness to seek the purpose and destiny for your life. Remember that you must have some type of interaction with God to receive a release from Him. So, basically, what I'm saying is that a relationship with our Savior must be established. Know that this relationship is not made by just going to church on Sunday – it is the time that is spent praying and worshiping, the study of the Word of God, and the sacrifices that you make concerning the things of the kingdom.

The time you spend with the Father, especially studying His Word, gives God time to release His revelations to you concerning your identity. This also allows God to kill your flesh so that you will start speaking and thinking through the Holy Spirit. When this happens, your mindset will start to shift, so how you see yourself will also change. This first step was the hardest for me because it took so much discipline, but this also jumpstarted my transition into a search for true identity and destiny. It was during this time that God sung over me that many are called but He chose me by name. The hardest part was not going back to my old ways and my old thinking.

During this time, make sure you have a strong prayer life. Ask God for you not only to be made over but to forget everything you have that will hinder you from finding your identity and moving forward in your purpose. Know that you will never be able to fulfill your assignment given by God if you can't or just don't understand who you are.

Many days, you will ask yourself if you are worthy of the calling that God has placed upon your life. It will seem unreal that God chose you, and you will know or feel that you are not qualified for what God has purposed you to be. How do I know this? It's because I felt this way, even after studying the Word. I remembered all of my past and knew God could not use me, or at least that's what I thought! I was my own worst enemy, and no one and nobody could tell me differently, not even God Himself. I was back again, wasting years of time because even though the Word said I was made in the image of God, I allowed my old mindset to creep back up on me.

I can say that during this part of the process, it was hard to say yes because I felt uneasy. But believe me, the Yes that

God was requiring opened up many doors that I was not even qualified for. Only God was able to release those locked doors. There were also many doors that were shut in this process; friends and family walked away during this time, and I felt so alone. Now, when I look back, I can see how the separation was needed, but when I was going through it, I didn't understand. It felt like I was being punished, but it was part of being refined. To be refined, you must go through some fire. This is when you have to depend on only Him and no one else, and you will learn how to tap into the strength you never knew you had. The Bible verses that you have been studying will now be so real to you in this part of the process, and life as you know it will start to change forever.

For me, this was a time when the enemy was trying to use depression to stop me from moving forward in seeing my identity. The enemy almost won, but God reminded me once again to begin to speak life over myself. He reminded me that I was more than a conqueror, and He let me know that even though I felt alone, He was with me all the time. During this time in the process, my trust level in God went to a different realm in Him. This was the time when He was preparing me. He wanted me to depend on no one but Him, and that is exactly what I did. This time, I didn't wait years – I did it suddenly. This is the time when I started to distinguish the voice of God from the voice of the world.

This is the turning point in this process, because God starts to trust you more with His mysteries, He has concerning your life. This is the time when you come to realize that your past does not determine your present, it was just a stepping stone to your next. You will understand that God has begun to turn a mess into a prize, and that you are God's prize. This is also the moment when you will realize that you were created for such a time as this, to experience the fullness of God. In this part of the process, you will start to see that Victory is who you are and not something that you will eventually become. You will start to believe that what God has for you is *for you*, and no one else will be able to fill your shoes because they only fit your feet. You start to become who you are in this part of the process.

During this time, which wasn't easy, I used prayer to get myself through. I would often say this prayer to myself, and it helped me to understand that I was made for a purpose:

> Heavenly Father, I, [state your name], praise you with all my heart. You are my shield, I take refuge in you all the days of my life, and I am safe. Even when the enemy comes like a flood, Lord, you have set a standard over my life, and you always remain victorious. I call to you, Lord, for you are worthy of my praise, and I am saved. In my distress, I can call unto you, for I know this battle is Yours and

not mine. Reach from on high and draw me out of all my troubles. Thunder from heaven, shoot your arrows and rout my enemies. Help me to walk in victory. In Jesus' name, thank you for dying on the cross for me. It is because of your great sacrifice that I am set free from the control of the enemy. Though I am broken and shattered on the inside, I stand firm in that completion that you have given me, and I declare and decree that nothing will take me down. I choose to walk in victory, for you have planted me on solid ground. The devil has nothing on me, for I am bought at a price. I will accomplish the purpose that God has for me. In Jesus' name!

That season was hard for me. It felt like I was repeating the same cycles over and over again. Sometimes I felt like giving up because my enemies seemed stronger than I. But the Bible says that greater is He who is in me than he who is in the world (1 John 4:4). Nothing is too complicated for our God. During this time, I would speak over myself words like this:

When the storm seems so fierce, remind me how great you are, my God. When the enemy fills my mind with fearful thoughts, it reminds me that he is just a created being. Fill me with strength, that I may stand and walk in victory. Let hope fill my heart so that I can rise and stand firm in your promises. In Jesus' name, cleanse me from anything that is blocking me from walking in victory. Fill me with peace and joy. Renew my strength so that I can soar like an eagle. May I run and not grow weary, may I walk in your ways and not fall. Help me to handle the challenges of my life with boldness because I am more than a conqueror through Christ Jesus. Keep my lamp burning and turn my darkness into light. Lord, your ways are perfect, and your words are flawless. I love and adore you. In Jesus' name. God, do not let me be ashamed. Arise from your throne and destroy all the enemies of my soul. Arm me with strength and help me to walk in the perfection that comes from Christ. I stand firm in the shield of victory that you have given me. By the authority that you have given me, I command my enemies to turn back in flight. I declare confusion in their camp, in Jesus' name. I praise you, for you are the God that defends me, in Jesus' name.

This prayer was used when I felt defeated or just needed encouragement to keep pushing. Never in a million years would I have believed it would be such a journey to find me. But I can tell you it was worth it, and it still is. I now know that I'm all that God has called me to be and much more. He created me to push past my emotions and thoughts, to receive all He has for me, and that is why this prayer was created. It reminded me to always keep my ears and heart open and empty for God to speak to me. I know that it took a lot of praying and fasting to receive answers, but more so for me to be emptied of the world and filled with the Holy Spirit. I do not want you to believe by any means that this is a fast or easy process, but I want you to understand that it is necessary and worth it all.

God gave us access to many things upon this land, and one of them is the authority to dominate and possess the land. But how can you possess something that you don't understand or believe you have access to? During this time, you will feel torn – it is actually a feeling that you can't explain. Something feels like it's missing in your life and hard to pinpoint, but you have a longing to fulfill. This is called fulfilling your purpose. This is the time in the process when you are not satisfied with the same old things. Not being in the will of God convicts you. I know this place all too well. Just know this is the time when that separation pays off. You now understand you are set apart to do the works of the Father. You will start to make others around you uncomfortable because you are starting to see yourself as God sees you. I was mad when it first started to happen, but now I see it as an honor.

You also have to understand that none of this journey is about your feelings – it's all about the call and purpose that God has for your life. There is a process of being emptied of all the toxicity that were placed upon you by this world. This is when pressure is applied and it feels as if life as you know it is slipping away. Close friends, family, and even you will question your church alignment. This will be the time when people in your life will tell you it doesn't take all that. They will let you know that they miss the old you, or they'll tell you the reasons why they can't support you anymore. Know that this is a tactic of the enemy to get you back into your same old mindset.

Let me be the first to tell you that God is on your side and the enemy can't win. This is the time in the process when you need to stay focused on God, and only on God. There will be light at the end of even the darkest tunnel. That's why I told you earlier that God had to help me to hear His voice over the voices of others, because it is during this time that doubt sets in. So, the words "victory," "overcomer," and "conqueror" must always be in the forefront of your mind. This is one of the biggest reasons why I made the statement that knowing who you are will come easier when you know who you belong to. You belong to Jesus – that name alone should say it all.

Let me show you who you are attached to. He is the Almighty One, our Alpha and Omega. He is the Anointed One, our Author and Perfecter of our Faith, the One who is our Beginning, the One who keeps our souls, our undefeated champion, the Bread of Life, our Comforter, the One who delivers. He is our Foundation, not just our Good Shepherd but our Great Shepherd, the One who guides us. He is the Head of this Church, the great I Am, Jehovah, the Light of the World, the Lion of the Tribe of Judah, the Lord of Lords, your Master, the Messiah, Mighty God, the greatest Physician, the Prince of Peace, the Mighty Transformer.

You belong to a Son who died but, best of all, got up so that you may have everlasting life. It should be so easy to find your identity just by checking God's record, especially because you carry His DNA. You belong to one who has given you the authority to step on the heads of the enemy. God is the one who reminds you that no one and nothing can stand in between you and your divine destiny. You have been given all the access you need to have victory, moment by moment, by the power of the Holy Spirit. There has been a portal opened over your life to receive from the Lord, and God Himself has set it in place. You just have to embrace what is ahead and never look at what is behind you. If you just remember that your past helped to get you to your present situation, you will embrace it even more. Your speech will start to change. You will start to become instead of just being!

# CHAPTER 2

# GOD, PLEASE ORDER MY STEPS

There are steps to carrying out the process of finding your identity and having a complete understanding of it. It is difficult, especially when you don't know where to start. Usually, it starts with going through a sanctification process. This part of the process is to gain an understanding of why you must be cleansed so you can hear from God clearly. You must be willing to allow your steps to be ordered, and the only way for this to happen is to empty yourself. God uses this act of sanctification as an act of submission. As I move forward, let me explain to you what sanctification is: it is an action of setting something or someone apart as holy, purifying it, and dedicating it to God's service. The Bible states that without holiness, no one will see the Lord (Hebrews 12:14). You really need God's sanctifying grace to be made holy, as God is holy. The Bible teaches us that God calls for His people to be holy. He sanctifies us from sin and empowers us to serve Him through faith and obedience. Sanctification is the process of becoming more like Christ in our conduct and character. So, this means that your lifestyle must mimic the ways of the Father. You should never look like the world, because others need to see that you are set apart. The way you conduct your life shows your walk or level with the Father – or your lack thereof.

This was a struggle for me for a long time because I didn't understand the full purpose of being sanctified, and also because I didn't realize that good character is what is done when no one is looking. Remember, I struggled with accountability, and during this part of the process, the enemy was using this against me. I was willing to be set apart, but only on my conditions – this was another setback for me. To be truly set apart is serious and nothing to play with, but I didn't see it that way.

I felt like God had to start me all over. During this time, I was going through a lot of health issues, and because of that, I was not as connected to God – I was letting the enemy in my head. But God once again reminded me to go back to speaking positive words over my life, and again my focus was clear and I was back on track. Now it was time to work on my character.

Sanctification plays a big part in your character. Your character is what is in your heart. It shows if you are mean spirited or if you share the heart of the Father. So, because of this, others will see you how God sees you. Good character allows you to carry yourself to a place where sin will no longer be an option. Good character allows God to clean you up so you will begin to handle situations and issues in the ways of the kingdom. I could go on and on in speaking about character, because I never believed that I had any character flaws, but guess what – I did. And God was working around the clock to show me how to fix different parts of my character. One of the biggest character flaws I had was speaking directly what was on my mind. God is love, and I wasn't displaying God's love through that flaw in my character. Because God is love, there is no way you can lack love and still believe you have good character. So, in this process, God revealed to me that character flaw and offered some correction – it was hard for me to receive it, but I was ready to move forward, and God was ready for me to move forward. This sanctification process was used to help me take on the mind of Christ and not only to live for Him but to live with Him!

Attitude is another vital part of sanctification and consecration. This is the turning point for how quickly or slowly you will find your true identity. God looks at motives and agenda. Your attitude will determine how you receive revelation and correction from the Father. You have to want to go beyond what your eyes can see and beyond your natural thinking. How you accept the information that is given to you will launch you into your next. You must also open yourself to follow so that God can lead. This comes with an attitude of always remaining teachable and understanding that to be a leader, you must first know how to follow. I never struggled with this part of the process, because I always believed that our posture was to be at the feet of God, and as He pours, we will receive. But I did have to adjust my attitude to how I received corrections. I was always one to explain why I was right or wrong instead of just taking the correction and working on it. Again, another stumbling block, but God never left my side. Your attitude can shut every door that God opens. Make sure you allow God to work on it.

Ostis B. Wilson, Jr., writes about sanctification:

> Sanctification is a grace that effects the inner man in such a way that his affections are alienated from the love of the world and exalted to a supreme love of God. The sanctified person loves the Lord with his whole heart, soul, mind, and strength (Mark 12:30). *"The love of God is shed abroad in our hearts by the Holy Ghost which is given unto us"* (Romans 5:5). When we receive the Holy Spirit and He sheds abroad the love of God in our hearts, then *"our love is made perfect"* (1 John 4:17). In such a state of

divine love (perfect love) there is no place for the least bit of anything contrary to love itself. Hence we are able to love our enemies (Matthew 5:44). Sanctification is also the perfecting of holiness in us. *"Having therefore these promises, dearly beloved, let us cleanse ourselves from all filthiness of the flesh and spirit, perfecting holiness in the fear of God"* (2 Corinthians 7:1).[1]

The website *Bible Lyfe* further describes the role of sanctification in the Bible:

God is holy and calls his people to be holy. Holiness is the attribute of God that binds all others together. Holiness does not define God's character, rather God's character defines what it means to be holy. God is holy. Holiness is godliness. Sanctification is the process of becoming holy like God. The following Bible verses about Holiness help us to understand God's character and our calling.

[...]

Leviticus 19:1-2 *"And the Lord spoke to Moses, saying, 'Speak to all the congregation of the people of Israel and say to them, you shall be holy, for I the Lord your God am holy.'"*

Leviticus 20:26 *"You shall be holy to me, for I the Lord am holy and have separated you from the peoples, that you should be mine."*

Matthew 5:48 *"You therefore must be perfect, as your heavenly Father is perfect."*

2 Corinthians 7:1 *"Since we have these promises, beloved, let us cleanse ourselves from every defilement of body and spirit, bringing holiness to completion in the fear of God."*

Ephesians 4:1 *"Even as he chose us in him before the foundation of the world, that we should be holy and blameless before him."*[2]

Reading these scriptures and truly understanding them, I then realized that there were many ways to help myself to live a sanctified life, but they first started with disconnecting from sin and allowing myself to be usable in the kingdom of God. This journey showed me that sin was easy to find and hard to let go of, and without rebuke and casting it away, it would never go on its own. "If you don't rise up against it, it won't go. You can wait from now till eternity for sin to go; but until you rise up against it, it won't. This is because it is determined to destroy your destiny."[3]

The funny part is that sin is bad but it often feels good – that is why we must resist sin. This is one reason why God sanctifies us to Him, because we receive extra strength to resist the enemy, which is sin. Remember, the Bible tell us that the enemy comes to steal, kill, and destroy (John 10:10), and this is the enemy's main job. Let me be the first to tell you that God is not the one who has put sin into your life; that is of the enemy, and you must cast that spirit away. If you don't, it will stand in the way of you finding your God-given destiny and purpose. His Word says that whosoever is born of God does not sin, because the seed of God abides in that person (1 John 3:9).

You must begin to use your mouth to decree and declare God to have complete power over your life. This is part of allowing the Holy Spirit in. David Oyedepo says:

> To live a sanctified life, you must learn to engage the power of the tongue. *"Death and life are in the power of the tongue: and they that love it shall eat the fruit thereof"* (Proverbs 18:21). So, your mouth is a weapon of war, and when you engage the power of the tongue, you can bring down your Goliath. What you don't declare, God has no legal right to confirm (Isaiah 44:26). [...] Engage the Spirit of love: There is a Spirit of love, which we can engage to conquer sin (Romans 5:5). So, when the Spirit of love dominates your life, you think no evil; you are free from evil acts. Love thinks no evil (1 Corinthians

13:5). So, engaging in the Spirit of love is one way to live a sanctified life. That Spirit of love is simply the Spirit of obedience. Engage the weapon of fasting: Through fasting, we destroy the yoke of filthiness. You can destroy anything that wants to destroy your life, through the weaponry of fasting (Isaiah 58:6).[4]

*"To God's elect [...] chosen according to the foreknowledge of God the Father, through the sanctifying work of the Spirit, to be obedient to Jesus Christ and sprinkled with his blood."* (1 Peter 1:1-2, NIV)

Kurt Selles writes:

God loves us so much that even before we were born, he chose us to be his children. After we were born, despite our desire to reject him, God sprinkled us with the blood of his Son, Jesus, and redeemed us. Now he wants us to live for him. [...] Our participation in this can be described mainly as obedience. Sanctification is the moment-by-moment process by which we more and more submit our hearts, minds, and bodies to following Jesus. [...] Thank God that the Holy Spirit sanctifies us by working in and through us! The Holy Spirit has not only set us free from sin but also lives in our hearts and reminds us to follow Jesus more closely. As we daily follow Jesus, we become holy, set apart for serving God.[5]

This is the place where our Savior wants you. Not only will He start to reveal your identity, but during this time, you will see that the way you function is different. Our Father will remind you that He qualifies those whom He calls. Because of this part of the process, the cleansing, God gives us instructions to follow to help us toward our next stage. We are to be:

- Quick to listen (hear the hearts of our brothers and sisters)

- Slow to speak (not everything needs a response)

- Slow to anger (think what would happen if God got mad at all the things you did, knowingly and unknowingly, without the facts)

- Quick to forgive (just like how on the cross, right before He died, Jesus said, "Forgive them, for they know not what they do")

Know that God understands you, even though everyone else may not. He loves you, and He commands you to love others as He loves you. Know that love covers hurt, and a multitude of sin (1 Peter 4:8).

God will remind you that you must get out of your emotions. His soft voice will whisper to you that your identity is a ministry, and it is not about you – it is for those who rely on you to complete their destiny. Basically your emotions must die daily, so you don't stand in the way of what God has for you.. Know that your character and integrity speak volumes! Your past doesn't determine your future, which means your condition doesn't determine your conclusion. In God, it doesn't matter how you fell down; it only matters how you get up. You know that your condition is just a state of being, but your conclusion is to come into what has already been given to you. When God is building your character, you must go through a time of correction, and you must mature to listen. It's already a tough process, but it can be a longer one if you are not open to change or are not surrounded by wise leaders who are not afraid to tell you the truth.

The next part of this process is called the crushing process, which helps you to develop the fruit of the Spirit. You must have the fruit of the Spirit before any gift of the Spirit can come. I remember when I heard a prophet say, "Truth doesn't always make you happy, but truth will make you free." No one wants to go through the process, but it's necessary. You can't desire the anointing but try to skip the process. You see the glory, but do you have what it takes to go through the process? Developing the fruit of the Spirit is a process. The more you seek your identity and your God-given destiny and purpose, the more God will pass over others to bless you by revealing His mysteries to you. Realize that only a Father identifies the cry of His own among all other cries.

So, because God chose you, He is calling you back to Him, and He is calling for you to get ready.

The more you seek your identity, the more God will shine upon you. Eyes have not seen nor have ears heard the greatness that God has for you. Your best is yet to come, your latter will be greater than your past, and you shall live to see it.

During this process, God will give you direct instructions, but He will also send confirmation to you through wise counsel. So, in this time, it is vital that you stay in alignment with God and with those He places to help you throughout this journey. Obedience is the key during this time – it shows God that you are willing to submit to and live under His guidance. Alignment is the key to staying under the will of God. It is the access to open the door to your God-given destiny and purpose.

If I can be transparent, nothing was going well in my life until I decided to submit under God's will even when it was painful to do so. Just as recent as the loss of my mom, I was in a very hurt, depressed place, and I didn't want to pray for myself – or anyone else, for that matter. God was still requiring me to work for Him in the kingdom, and I was barely standing. I now know that He was carrying me through the whole time. During the process God took me through, I was broken down and felt unworthy, but now I know that God had to break me down to build me up. He molded and shaped me to become a Son of the kingdom. Submission was the key. I had to give up the likes of me to look up to God and tell Him that He had full control to take charge of my life so I could live in the whole of Him. God replied to me, *"Be still and know that I am God"* (Psalm 46:10).

Karen Holmes notes that the phrase "be still" "is actually derived from the Hebrew word *rapha* which means 'to be weak, to let go, to release.' Essentially, it means surrender." I learned the truth that she describes: "When we surrender ourselves, our lives, our will, our desires, to Him, He is able to more fully reveal Himself to us and we are more able to fully experience Him." It helped me to "trust God enough to let go of those things [I was] clinging to so tightly, in order that [I] may know a more intimate relationship with Him."

As Holmes continues to reflect on this verse, she writes:

> *Surrender yourself in order that you may know that I am God...* your refuge; your strength; your present help in trouble; your comforter and King in uncertain times; your security; your center; your steadfast ruler; the commander of the universe; the Lord of Hosts; the God of Jacob; the Victorious One; the One before whom every knee shall bow, on earth and in Heaven.

Surrender... what does that mean? What does that even look like in real life? In war, surrendering means dropping your weapons, putting down your shields, forsaking your current leadership and its agenda and acquiescing to the will of another. To me, personally, surrendering looks like setting aside all the ways I protect myself and my pride, laying down those weapons that defend me against pain and criticism, and turning my back on all the idols I have allowed to have authority over my life: Pride. Shame. Envy. Pleasing Others. Fear of failure. [...] What if "being still," SURRENDERING, actually means giving up all attempts at self-preservation?[6]

I was only able to step into what God had for me because I wanted to change and was willing to change. God did this by first changing my mindset and how I thought about myself. God loved me past my failure, and that was just what I needed to push me beyond my own limitation. You cannot skip any part of the process of sanctification because this is the only way you can fully embrace God's call upon your life. Sanctification is not done overnight as a matter of fact you must sanctify yourself daily to stay cleansed and usable. Once you get through this part of the process of finding your true identity, what is left to follow in the process will seem like a breeze.

- CHAPTER 3 -

# It's Time to Grow Up

As the process continued, I felt like I was having an out-of-body experience. There were days when it felt like I was watching myself but couldn't control what was going on with me. I was no longer the same. I would say now that it was a good thing, but at the time, I didn't like that I wasn't in control anymore – God was the leader, and I just had to follow. I had no other choice; I was no longer given the option. All of the hard work was paying off, but I knew there was still more to come. God was working on my state of mind; my thinking was no longer about what I was, but about who I was becoming. Transformation was a must and was happening suddenly. God made it His business to work on my attitude, which helped me to receive not only correction but revelation in a different way. I learned that my emotions have nothing to do with the call that God has on my life. God often told me to get out of my feelings, that I could no longer trust my flesh. I would never have believed that this journey would lead me to where I am today. I now walk in the office of the Prophet, married to an amazing husband of 18 years. I'm a mom of two adult children, with a career as a general manager, and I'm now being pushed out of my comfort zone into my next. It seems like the journey never ends. I guess when we leave this earth is when we take our rest – other than that, we work.

My talk was no longer the same – I adopted the language of God. I didn't hang out at the same places I was before. It just didn't feel right anymore. My circle began to get really small; I hung around with people who were where I was going, and I was no longer the smartest one in my group. I remember having a strong desire to make Jesus proud of me. I finally was able to look in the mirror and see myself as God saw me – a feeling that I would never forget. The more I reminisce, the more I see that this was a time when I was becoming: God became my potter, and I yielded to be the clay. He was the puppet master, and I was the submitted puppet. I was becoming a great mother, a wife, an amazing child of God, one whose past didn't determine my future. I begin to answer the call to preach and teach. I was anointed to gather the lost souls that God called me to. I was chosen to go after the 1 while the 99 stayed together – what an honor. When I looked up my identity, it was looking back at me. I was finally walking into my purpose and accepting my kingdom assignment, no longer hiding and running because of fear of the unknown. Guess what, it only took 15 years. I know that I wasted so much time not believing that God wanted to use me, and the other part of the time, I was allowing people to tell me I wasn't ready and believing them. But can I tell you that the more I was told I couldn't, the more I did.

This process was long and painful. There were times when I was mad at God because I didn't understand why He had placed his mandate upon me. When I step back and think of what I was and who I am now, I can't help but praise God! I finally love the "me" I see, and you will love the "you" you see also. Do not grow weary in your test. This is just your preparation for your greater.

I am the one who actually told God I was ready to find who I was, not knowing that it would take a complete process. Make sure that before you say yes, you really mean it. I was determined to find my identity, to function in what God has for me. This process is never finished; that is why you must die to yourself daily and always remain teachable. During this beginning process, I had to totally commit to killing my flesh before it raised up. This transformation changed my entire life, and it started with one yes – the one without conditions.

The new me is more than looks – it is confidence and boldness, basically saying that now I know who I am because I know whose I am. Then I look back now, I can see why you can't skip any parts of the process. There must be a foundation laid so that if you ever have a setback, you have knowledge to fall back on.

One of the important parts of this process that I haven't discussed yet was God telling me that it was time to grow up. I replied to God, "Grow up? I'm raised with two children, a husband, and a promising career. I lead workers at a great job," and God said, "With all of that, you still need to grow up." This was one of the biggest pieces of my transformation, and I'm still a work in progress. The growing up was not about what I was going through or what I was willing to sacrifice, but it was how I responded to situations. God wanted to teach me self-control. He also helped me to understand that not every person or every situation was my assignment, and that I needed to stop filling my schedule with things that are not part of my assignment.

I often received the correction in my carnal mind and not with the mind of Christ; this was proof that I did need to mature. This started to happen again to me recently after the passing of my mom. I was so hurt and was allowing grief to overtake me. I had to realize that maturing was not something that happened instantly but something you must continue to work at, because we grow every day. Maturing allows God to trust you with the hard things, and it helps you trust God to solve the problem. It becomes a relationship: there is a call-and-response that takes place. There were certain parts of finding my identity that blessed my life because I learned so much more and grew up suddenly. You have to be a willing participant, though. The part of maturing prepared me for the transition of my parents. Remember, God knows the plans He has for you; He has said He would never harm you but will give you a bright future (Jeremiah 29:11). This part of the process is necessary but hard. I will continue to say that it is worth it.

I have never known anyone to wake up and say that they want to go to war, but many people do say that it is time for a change. Change is an action word – it's not something that just comes, but something that takes work. Hard work! There is one reward for following the path that God has placed before you: change! You will realize that you are becoming. Your eyes will be wide open to the call on your life. No longer can you be manipulated into thinking you are not God's chosen. You will finally know you are strong enough to encourage others by your transformation.

Even through this part of the process, I came to a time when I had to demand my soul to follow the will of God. It became a daily prayer that came from following God even when I didn't understand the vision He had for my life. I learned to worship even when things were going badly. I was always reminded that I had never arrived but that I was still arriving. The advice I would give you is to continue to be God-led: don't move before Him, and make sure you are not too far behind Him. Don't get discouraged by what God is requiring of you, but be honored that He is requiring it from you. Don't let past trauma be part of present and future actions and success!

I remember that during this process, there were certain times when God allowed me to see what was waiting for me due to the call on my life. God had those who were called or assigned directly to me. Through dreams and visions, God would show me bits and pieces of His plans for me. I believe He used that to keep me focused and in alignment with Him. It was a big world that was waiting for me to find who I was so that others would be able to find who they were. I came to realize that this journey I was on had nothing to do with me – it had to do with those who were called to my life. Also, I do want to share that those people were not always in a church setting. God used my job as a platform for ministry. That is why I had to be set apart from the world to have a heart and mind of Christ. God was sending me into the world to change and shift. There was no way I could be of the world. I remember being in church one time and hearing the voice of God say to me that if I continued to submit, He would send me to the nations. He did just that. I still believed that I was not prepared to teach or to deliver God's words to a group of people, but at the moment I was doing so, it didn't feel as bad, and I wasn't as nervous. I started to remember the process. God was preparing me for these very moments.

If I could share anything with you today, it would be not to give up. There is a bigger picture that God is making you a part of, and it will be mind-blowing. The doors that opened in my life were amazing, but I missed many of my blessings because I didn't know how to treat them. I want you to know that you were chosen before you were formed in your mother's womb. You were already mandated to be a force upon this earth, so fear should never stand in the way. You have a part in the world, and without your part, the world would never be complete. This was becoming so real to me, and that is how I had to start seeing things.

I had many heartbreaks; many people turned their backs on me, and it was hard to bounce back from it. At one point in my life, I felt that if I laid down who God called me to be, I would be happier. I was never satisfied; I felt like something was always missing. I was depressed and never able to find that happiness I was searching for until I turned back to my Father to receive it. It was hard for me to understand that God said I was part of a royal priesthood when I didn't feel like it. I did everything under the sun to be unholy, and God still wanted to use me. So, when I turned back to Him, that is when I felt whole and complete. Not to pressure you, but when my walk changed, everything that was attached to me changed. My eyes were opened in a different way: they were now wide open.

I cared about who I hung out with, the places I was going, the things I was doing. I looked at the way I was living my life differently. I really started to care, what would Jesus think with every decision I made. People who paid me no mind before were asking me to pray for them, and it was a form of respect that I know I did not establish. It caused me to carry myself in a different way, and also to see myself in a different way – I started to see myself the way God saw me, not the way the world saw me. It was part of my transformation. There were words that people would speak over my life, and I would respond to myself, "Yes, would always be the answer."

God transformed my insides, but now He wanted to work on my outside. The inner me had to meet the outer me, and again I wasn't ready. It was more than changing my hair or the way I dressed; it was a full and complete detox.

Remember, I used the word "determination" before, so now, I'm using the word "commitment." This is an action word, something that is easy to say but hard to do. This was a time in the process when God wanted me to submit to healthy living. It was my eating, allowing only positive things to be in my eye gates and allowing only positive things to come out of my mouth. Well, this was hard. I mean it – this was like torture. I was thinking, "What does losing weight and what I watch on TV have to do with knowing my identity?" Let me help you: it meant a lot. We often compare ourselves to what we see or who we hang around. What we say out of our mouths is often the issues we have on our hearts. So, until we stop allowing ourselves to be exposed to those very things, we cannot change who we are and step into what God wants us to be.

This is why God said we were to die to ourselves daily and that we must always remain teachable; we always have to be empty and open to receive. Revelation and correction are one and the same – we must always be open to change because knowing your identity means losing who you created to take on what God made you. Just imagine how far you could be today if you didn't waste time following your own voice or the voices of those in the world! Well, that is what happened to me. I lost about 20 years because I just didn't listen. And why? Even now I look back and know that I'm not where I was, but I'm still a long way from where I should be.

- CHAPTER 4 -

# THERE IS A COST TO YOUR MANDATE

I was so focused on finding my identity that I didn't focus on the plans of the enemy. This is real – the enemy is out to kill, steal, and destroy, especially when he doesn't want you to find your kingdom mandate. The enemy knows how powerful you would be if you only knew who you were. So, he is going to try to stop it from coming to pass by any means necessary.

The enemy came up against my health. It was hard for me to find my way. He was trying to work within my marriage, even trying to attack my children. It felt like I couldn't do anything to win. I felt so defeated, and the more I fought to stay focused, the more I wasn't. I had every excuse for why I was not winning. The enemy was using things that were close to me to hurt me, and I remember at one point just running and basically hiding myself. To the world everything seemed okay, because I was pretending, but I was spiritually dying on the inside. During this time in my process, I stopped attending church, I stopped tithing, and I even gave up the gift of dance. Basically, anything that was connected to God, I gave it up. I didn't want it anymore if that meant that the fight against me would stop.

God allowed my leader to see me slipping away, and I was confronted. I explained what was going on with me and how I felt. I remember the words that were being told to me – to just run into the presence of God. I was told that I needed to have more time with the Holy Spirit. I was told to allow the Spirit to lead me and to stop trying to do it on my own strength. That was when I was able to open up my Bible once again. I began to start declaring and decreeing over myself that I should live to see the works of the Lord. I had to remind myself often that I was more than a conqueror. This was the time when God Himself told me that I was the apple of His eye. I knew I can do all things though Christ; I was just having a hard time finding my way back to Him. I truly understand that statement now. Without God, we are nothing; He is the very air we breathe.

If I can share this with you, when I truly connected to Christ, whatever I set out to do was completed and I prospered from it. There is a blessing in obedience. I stress to you the time I had lost by not believing the word of God, which caused me not to have confidence in myself. But I also want to reveal to you that there has been a blessing in my waiting. I recall the process of being pregnant: without going through the whole process, the baby would not have been fully developed. The process was long and painful, but I received a beautiful baby in the end.

If I had been released too soon into my assignment, I could have gotten hurt, or I could have hurt someone. I knew my mindset wasn't where it needed to be mentally; I wasn't ready to walk in my purpose, and I knew I would not have been effective. We can't rush the process – only God can do that. In this day and age, people skip over so much in the process, and when their back is against the wall, they just give up. There are many levels to finding your identity: not just discovering what it is and walking in it but also being effective in what and who you are called to be. I have watched many people who were close to me not be effective because once they believed they had found their purpose, they just forgot about God and moved in their own spirit.

In the process, you will have many regrets, but I was ultimately able to make them lessons learned. I would not have made it without God. When you are ready to transform, please make sure that you have those walking with you who are God-ordained to do so. Make sure they are called to push you out of your comfort zone. When you think of a mentor, know that they are there to tell you when you are not right or if you are falling out of alignment with God. You must also trust the God in those who are called to walk with you; if you don't, you will never be able to accept the correction from them, because you won't believe the correction is coming from God. That would cause you to question their motives or agendas toward you. It would not be worth your time to entertain someone you don't trust.

The easiest thing you can do is to pray and ask God to show you "you." That sounds crazy, but it works – it helps you to see what you would never have known on your own. I remember when God exposed me to me; I wasn't ready for it. He showed me things about myself that I never thought were bad. Can I tell you that this was the first time I told God I didn't believe my ways were wrong? Can I tell you that I lost the fight? God told me to change or else, with a period at the end.

There is a cost to your mandate: it is lots of sacrifices. Let me explain to you the meaning of this word. The dictionary defines a mandate as "an official order or commission to do something." It gives you "the authority to carry out a policy or course of action, regarded as given by the electorate to a candidate or party that is victorious in an election."[7]

I always heard the word "mandate" but never truly understood the meaning of it, so we know that I didn't understand the cost that it carried. To whom much is given, much is required (Luke 12:48). I guess I had watched so many other people walk in their mandate, and they made it look very easy. Well, God allowed me to get a taste of what the cost of the mandate looks like. I do know that the reason why God revealed my God-given destiny and purpose before He had begun to apply lots of pressure to me was because He didn't want me to give up.

It seems like when I looked up, I was losing people around me, including family and friends – my whole support system was turning away from me. God said this was the time He wanted me to depend only on Him. There were times when I couldn't go out to hang out because God would have me stay home and pray. He would have me use that time to concentrate on Him. It's all part of identity. You must be empty before the Lord to be filled up.

The other part of this process is giving you time and money toward the mandate. What you put in is what you get out of anything you are doing. Sowing is part of honor and reverence to God. This is a part of the process that can't be skipped over. God uses this time for you to plant seeds that will grow as you mature in your walk. The biggest part of the process that I remember was when I had to give up who I was to pick up the hearts of those God had called me to. I want to share with you that I experienced this act with someone who had hurt me prior, and God still sent me to serve them.

God wants to make your skin like rubber, because there is a lot of backbiting, and this walk is already lonely. That's why I said that you should only build God-based relationships. Many people don't understand the vision or your purpose, so they try to make you believe that you are crazy. That's when I learned to stop giving my vision to blind people, those who can't see beyond their own desires. God will call you to minister to the same people who hurt you; the only advice I can give you is to remember that obedience is better than sacrifice. It is hard to pray or be there for someone who has hurt you, but the Word does say that God will make your enemies your footstool (Psalm 110:1). The Bible also says 44 [a]But I say to you, (A)love your enemies, bless those who curse you, (B)do good to those who hate you, and pray (C) for those who spitefully use you and persecute you, 45 that you may be sons of your Father in heaven; for (D)He makes His sun rise on the evil and on the good, and sends rain on the just and on the unjust.( Matthew 5:44, 45) This part of the process is called trial by fire – God wants to make sure you are ready!

You must discern the difference between the voice of God and the voice of the world. Because of the process you are going through, the enemy sends assignments to people to bother you and make you give up on seeking your identity. Not keeping my guard up, I allowed the enemy to cause me to fail many times because the voice of God was overpowered by the voices of others telling me that I was never going to be who God predestined me to be. I had many losses during this time, but when I look back, I see that those connections were not in the will of God. He who is not called will never understand the cost of walking in your kingdom mandate.

It felt like the closer I got to my purpose, the more I was told by God to take the money from my family's livelihood to invest it in the assignment. I noticed that the time I would usually spend with my family was being sacrificed. There were times when I had to be strong enough to minister to others when everything around me was going wrong.

As God was maturing me, I had to be strong enough to encourage others that God would solve their problems, even when He had not solved mine yet. I was betrayed by the people I helped, and I still had to love them and pretend like I was never hurt. I was abandoned by the people who swore to never leave me. I had to forgive so my blessings wouldn't be blocked. I remember the time when people stopped respecting me because they were poisoned by other people who teamed up with others just to go against me. I had fake people in front of me, calling me "sister" and disrespecting me behind my back.

Some people misinterpreted things I said, thinking it was indirectly said about them. There was a time when everything I said and did was a problem to someone. This journey was long and lonely. There were many days when I begged God for some type of relief. There were times when I had to stand there as people disrespected my husband and family. There were many people who questioned my motives and believed I had a hidden agenda, even though I knew this was not true.

There were many stories made up about me, and if I'd had low self-esteem, it could have taken me over the edge. Thank God for Jesus! Know that the enemy can't do anything that God does not allow him to do. Many people walked with me until they thought that I was receiving too much attention. I gave many platforms to people who tried to crush the vision God gave me. So, because God allowed these things to happen, I had to remain prayed up and under the Holy Spirit. God used those situations to bring me closer to Him. During this time, I also had to tell myself not to make excuses or apologies for my anointing, gifts, talents, opportunities, advancement, elevation, and calling! I reminded myself that if GOD wanted to hide me, HE WOULD; when HE wanted to PROPEL me, HE did just that! I don't have to be embarrassed, ashamed, or TIMID when GOD told me to COME ON! I would often apologize for who I am in God. I had to keep telling myself to go ahead and do what I have been CHOSEN to do!

So now I'm talking to YOU! While naysayers stay busy flapping their gums against you, they will have to sit and watch YOUR dream manifest while theirs fail to get past a second thought! Throughout this journey, I came to realize that adults need villages too, not just children. So, I chose to surround myself with good people. You need to do the same too! Seeking your identity will cause you to do a lot of housekeeping when it comes to your circle of friends or associates.

Excuses will always be there, but it is up to you to stay focused, because opportunity won't always be knocking at your door. Your success is a direct result of the actions you take or the excuses you give. We allow everything under the sun to stop us from doing the things of the kingdom, yet we show up to work every day. We give no effort but expect great results. We have to stop doing life the same way and expecting different results. When you seek to change, you will. When you seek your identity and you are determined, you press. Even when it hurts, press; even when you feel weary, press. God will see your pressing and carry you the rest of the way.

During this process, you will see others who seem to be going faster through their process, but please don't get jealous or envy them, because jealousy will have you gossiping about the people you should be learning from. That is why God said to love one other and have no issues with your brother or sister. You don't know their journey or what they had to sacrifice throughout their walk. We block our own blessings all the time by wanting something that God didn't give to us yet.

As you go with this process, make sure you write and allow God to guide your words through declarations such as:

Lord, I thank you for every gift you have given me. I declare I will not be the servant who buried his talents anymore! That season is over! My goal in life is to live full and abundant and to die empty because my life is being poured out in worship and service to you. Lord, let me be a vessel you can use by your power and your Spirit.

Prayer is the key to relationships. It is also the way the Father hears you and hears your prayers. Believe it or not, through prayer and instruction God can even download a book. You must know that God speaks all the time and you have to be open to listen. That is why it is always good to have a pad and pen with you at all times, which will also help with the process. Throughout this whole process, you will be given instructions, and you will need to follow them even if it doesn't make sense to you at the time. I have learned that when you think you have skipped over or gotten away with something you were instructed to do, God has a way of having you repeat the same test over and over again until you pass it. So, wouldn't it be great just to pass the test the first time? Just something for you to think about.

# CHAPTER 5

# I'M STILL STANDING

This process elevated my mind. It was unbelievable, the state of peace and boldness, of knowing that God created for me to be more than I could imagine I would ever have been on my own. I was God's Deborah here on earth. He handpicked me and was preparing me Himself. As I was becoming one with my identity, there were certain parts that stood out to me. I know I was called to set order, to make the way for Jesus' second coming. I was called to gather the people of God to return back to God's original blueprint for His people. All I could do was think about what an honor it was. The joy of the Lord absolutely became my strength.

In this part of the process, I had to keep myself emptied so God could speak to me and though me. This is not always easy, but I had to learn how to step out of my own way. No longer was it "I," but I began to look at God like I looked at my husband: we became one. There was nothing that could separate us. He had my back, and I wanted to please Him and show him I had His. So, the choices and the decisions I made were made to suit both of us. Could you imagine what I had to go through to be totally sold out for Jesus? I asked you that question because the more I found out who I was, the more I realized that I was truly becoming like my Abba. I only had one desire, and that was to please the Father!

The enemy was trying to break me down during this whole process; it felt like darts and bullets being thrown my way. The only thing I could do was bend and duck, but at one time, it felt like the enemy hit me so hard that I was knocked on my back. This happened when my mom passed away. I couldn't breathe, or maybe I just couldn't get over the fact that she was gone. I had many people around me, telling me once again how and what I needed to feel. So, I felt myself going back to my old ways of going into a cave alone and no longer expressing myself. I once again stepped away from my call. How did this happen once again?

There were decisions that had to be made; there was a reset that had to be done in my mind. As it happened, I realized it made no sense to go through the process and all the hell that I went through just to sit down on my gifts. I got such a reality check: every time it felt like I was going back under rubble,, God would pull me out and then allow me to lower myself back in the hole again. Even though I was making my bed, He wanted me to know that He was there with me but wanted me to make my own decisions. I knew God had sent me into this earth realm to be a world changer and an atmosphere shifter, and being ready was going to take much more than just saying I was ready. Preparation is what takes place prior to being called; it doesn't happen while you are on the front line. Through all the battle scars, it was time for me to launch out and complete what I was sent to do, which was to process and dominate my sphere of influence. Remember, I told you that God whispered to me that He was sending me to the nations. Now I am ready. I anticipate the when and where, and I can only imagine what God has in store for me.

During this time, I can sense the feeling of having a renewed heart. I'm now quick to forgive the wrongs that were done to me – how could I not? God has never held anything I have done in the past against me; my wrongs were washed away and I was made whole. So, who am I to not forgive my brother or sister who made a mistake? During this process, I had to acknowledge that forgiveness is not for the other person, it is for me. I refuse to allow anger to block God from using me. If I held on to who and what had wronged me, I would never be able to worship God in Spirit and in truth.

My spirit is renewed. I can still hear the way I cried out to God, asking Him to make me over. He knew everything I was hiding, and He delivered me from everything and continued to make me usable. God allowed this time for me to sit for a while, and I was able to be restored. I was in counseling and just sitting under the word of God. I was being healed from the inside out. When your spirit is renewed by God, He pours power and anointing upon you like never before. The revelation you receive during this time is supernatural. It's a feeling that you can't explain, but you long for it. This caused me to give God an unconditional yes, withholding nothing. You are saying without using words, "Less of me and more of you, God. It's your will and not my will, God." The door is open for God to have full control. You must consider this part of the process an honor.

In this process, my heart was renewed. I know this was so because I no longer held on to past trauma. The feelings I had in my heart in prior years against people who had hurt me were no longer the same. I was actually able to see those same people now and even give them a hug. There was a time when people knew my triggers or how to open up old wounds. As far as I can remember, I was carrying a physical pain in my heart that was activated with sudden incidents in my life. When I think back, I can't even tell you the last time I sensed that feeling in my heart. God was allowing me to see what healing looks like. There is a peace that was placed upon me, and it was only God that could have given it to me. The transformation that was taking place was something that others saw with their natural eye, but my position was being changed in the spirit realm. When I think about it now, I still get teary eyed.

God sent a fresh wind of strength my way. This was another supernatural act of the Father. I could feel myself breathing in the wind of God and releasing the toxicity of the world in the same breath. This is when I understood that it was in God that I lived and had my being. I was being purified from the inside out. I felt like I was being cleansed through the wind. This same wind was blowing when I was going through trials and tribulations, not realizing it was a wind of strength. The wind to run the race, the wind that causes us to bend and bow but gives us the strength not to break. God was blowing His winds upon me from the East, West, North, and South. I received such a release of the Holy Spirit.

Let me be the first time to tell you that the time is now. It's time for you to step up and bust out. There is no better time to start this process than now. You must start to be the best "you" that you can possibly be. The world is changing, but God is still the same. You have no more time to waste. There is a world waiting for you to step into your destiny. This time is the right time. You will never be ready to start; you just have to jump into the unknown and allow God to lead you.

Let me be the first to tell you that God didn't only say these things to you: in the Bible, He told Abram to go and leave behind all that was familiar to him. I can picture your mind racing – you are saying, "I tried it before and it didn't work." But God has said that for you, it won't be the same the second time around. Allow Him to remake you. You won't think the same way, you won't talk the same way, life as you know it will change forever. You must just stay the course and not allow the cares of this world to stop you from your purpose. God is calling you to arise! Will you answer the call? You are being called out of every dry and stagnant place in your life. God is calling you higher in Him – no traditions or religion but just His presence. This is not the time to be fearful but the time to be bold. This is not the time to tuck yourself into a little box but the time to be limitless in the things of God.

Answer your call, stand up and arise. Is there a preacher, teacher, or dancer hidden in you? God tells us in the Bible that there is a treasure hidden inside of each and every one of us. I demand you open your eyes and pick up your mantle. Are you called to the White House or to be an ambassador to the nations? Or are you called to bring life to a dying world? Whatever it is, you need to seek and go after what is yours. Remember that what God has for you is only for you. It is time to reclaim your time and take back everything the enemy had tried to take for himself. Nothing in your life has happened by a mistake – just consider the mistakes lessons learned.

If I could share a testimony with you, during the parts of my journey that stood out and were changing points in my life, I had to press my way to finding my identity. Throughout my young life, I struggled with having lots of insecurities, which led to low self-esteem. This is what started a pattern in my life where I learned how to adapt to my surroundings. I had a lot of people in my life who would get close to me and then throw me away like trash. For a long time in my life, I was repeatedly going through the same cycles. Looking back at my teenage years, I was such a leader, people always followed me, but guess what – I followed the crowd. I never saw in myself what people saw in me. I always connected to the wrong people because I was intimidated by those who had confidence. I felt those were the ones who would eventually hurt me.

Now to my young adult years: I brought my childhood into my adult life, but I learned to maintain my peace even though I wasn't satisfied. I believe this was the time when I was trying to find my way and seek my identity, but because I didn't know who or what I was looking for, I took on the identity of others. I noticed that people enjoyed me more, or at least I thought so. If you are not who God called you to be, you will never be loved the way you need to be. I was married and a mom, but I was still seeking. That's when the partying started. I remember questioning myself, asking if this was truly me. I still wasn't satisfied. This was also during the time in my marriage when I basically didn't know if I still wanted to be a wife. During that time, I was working as an Emergency Medical Technician, and after 16 years, I no longer had a desire to work as an EMT. I struggled to stay at work and to be satisfied with it – again, this was me not knowing my identity. I went from day to day so unhappy and depressed, knowing that I was missing something in my life, but because I truly didn't care and didn't understand who God was, I did not know how to seek something that I did not know about. But one night, I went to a church service that I was invited to, and I saw a group of women dancing. That was the start of my walk with God.

Remember, I was a partier – I loved to dance, and God showed me that night that I can just trade partners. Through dance ministry, God started to process me through my journey with Him. For a long time, I believed I was only called to dance, but God used my boldness in Him to make me His mouthpiece. I recall a time when I was speaking and heard the voice of God coming through my voice box. That was the day that changed my life. It propelled me into my next, meaning my next level in God. Because of my willingness to seek after God, doors were opened that no man could close. I was placed on big platforms to deliver the word of God.

Then sickness came in – the enemy was at his job. Because of the process I had stepped into, my trust and faith were very strong. I believed He would heal me, and He did. I believed that God would trade my setback for a big comeback, and guess what, He did. During this process, God was trading my sorrows and pain for joy and prosperity. He took my ashes and placed beauty upon me. My life as I knew it was changing. God covered all my wrongs and did not show people the best parts of me; He dealt with me in our private time. I wouldn't want to lie to you and tell you that it was all good, because it wasn't. There was still hurt; there were times when I wanted to give up. God waited for me; some days, He was really close to me, and other days, He was very distant. Let me repeat what I said: God waited on me! There were times when God allowed me to make my own choices, and they were the wrong choices most of the time, but He still rescued me, especially after He made me sweat.

I learned that I needed to revere God more, even when things didn't go my way. I was instructed to worship God when I was hurting the most – to cry out to Him more and allow Him to wipe away the tears. I was put in many corners; my back was against the wall. But guess what – God always made a way. The process of getting to know who I belonged to was harder than getting to know who I am! Sometimes it was fun reading the Bible because it was stories, and at times, I could imagine myself in the Bible times. I remember reading the love stories of God and what He says about me. I could clearly hear Him speaking to me. The relationship that developed between the Father and me was amazing. I began to recognize His voice, and He knew mine.

My family wanted to know why I was so happy, and how my life had changed for the better. God used this very act to draw people to me; He caused them to be attracted to my anointing. God placed me with great leaders in my life, even great friends – and this time, I didn't have to be embarrassed to be around them. Do you believe I used to hide my friends from God? Sounds crazy, right? As I was being prepared, there were supernatural acts that were taking place in my life, such as being able to walk again after I was told I never would. I was told that my tongue would never move again for me to talk, but I'm talking.

I remember a time when my heart was beating 270 beats per minute and the doctor told me that he had to stop my heart or it would stop on its own, and I'm still here. Wouldn't you think it would have been time for me to find my purpose on this earth? God brought me through so much, and I know it wasn't for nothing. He was saving me for something special; that is why I had to wait to go through the process. What God had stored up in me took time to create – it wasn't just thrown together. I am His masterpiece put together by the greatest, and now I know! How about you?

The Word of God became a weapon I used in and out of season. I used the Word of God to stop the enemy from every angle. It was easy to do when I understood that the Word wasn't something that was written, it is what was promised by God. So, if God be for me, then who can stand against me? The hardest battle I ever had to fight was not fighting at all! I was reminded that the battle was not mine but the Lord's. So, every time the enemy tried to make me believe that God was not for me, I was reminded that God would never leave me nor forsake me. When trials were coming from every side, I remembered that if I had faith as little as a mustard seed, then I would be healed.

When people would tell me that I wasn't what I believed God called me to be, I reminded them that I was made in the image of the Father, and because He is, I am! The Word became a sword, and I was able to bring many mountains down by knowing the right words to pray and how to use them strategically and effectively. No longer was I bound to a place of insecurity; I was launched onto the front lines, and all I could use was my knowledge, my wisdom, and my mouth. I was able to confuse the enemy with my praise and make him angry with my worship. It was even better when my life started to manifest the life God had in store for me. The enemy used to try me for no reason, but like a tree planted by the water, I told the enemy that I shall not be moved. I was ready to be the best me I can be!

- CHAPTER 6 -

# CONCLUSION

In conclusion, I pray that this book has inspired you to launch into your next with the Father. We were promised to prosper and have a life that is full of joy. That is why God told us that those who wait on the Lord shall mount up on wings like eagles that soar. They shall walk and not be weary, and they shall run and not faint (Isaiah 40:31). There is a promise in the waiting. Let's continue to allow God to have full control over the steps we take. If God leads you and guides you along the way, I can promise you won't stray.

Realizing my identity in Christ was the best thing that could ever have happened to me. It launched me to opening up my wealthy place, especially when I remembered reading in the Bible that God had blessings stored up for me and my obedience would open the portal to be released over my life. If I could say anything about my life, I would tell you that I would not change it for the world.

Make sure you take time out of your busy schedule to have time for God. There are many things that God wants to share with you. A Sunday relationship won't do. When God opens your eyes to see yourself the way He sees you, things will never be the same. Eyes wide open will remind you that God knows all the plans He has for you, and this will launch you into your future suddenly. Make sure you don't allow pride to stand in your way. No one has ever made it to the top alone. God wants me to remind you to honor the leadership that He has placed over you – they are there for a reason. It will not always be cookies and cream. They are not there to tell you that everything you do is perfect, but they are there to perfect your gifts and to make you accountable for the choices you have made. They are there to assist you in your godly walk. Remember, if you don't trust the God in your leader, you need to disconnect, because it won't work. God's correction comes through the leader as confirmation, and you have to be ready to receive.

Transformation takes place when you are willing to change. You have to allow God to tap into the hidden places in your life, the places that you tucked so far away you forgot about them. A healing has to take place before you can truly be transformed. You can't skip any parts in the process that God is taking you through. The Word says to be anxious for nothing (Philippians 4:6). God wants me to remind you that there is a blessing in the pressing and healing in the waiting.

Made sure your eyes and ears stay open for God's next move. Eyes wide open will show you how God wants us to see things in the spirit realm and not in our flesh.

Pain fuels the pursuit of your purpose. Anything that is worth it is worth fighting for. So, let me be the first person to tell you that you are worth it. You're asking me how I know? Because our Savior thought you were worth dying for. I was propelled to look beyond what I could see and tap into what God wanted me to see. Life is truly like a box of chocolates, but with Jesus, you know whatever you get will be amazing.

God wanted me to use this book to let you know hat you are not alone. Everyone has a journey, but we are all going toward the same goal, and that is to fulfill our God-given destiny and purpose. God no longer wants us to leave this earth still pregnant with our purpose. You owe it to yourself to be the best you that you can be. If you never become who God called you to be, that something will always be missing. Once you know who God is and that He chose you, I can promise you that you will be excited to know who you are. Picture yourself falling in love all over again, but this time with yourself. Aren't you looking forward to that? It is an exciting journey.

I hope this book has given you some directions on where to start.

# AFTERWORD

I have had the pleasure of knowing and loving my Prophetess Tesha Williams-Hall since 2015, when we graduated from TEN Dance! When she walked into the room, you felt the presence of the Holy Spirit that surrounded her, and that light drew me to her. She's always been a humble, loving, compassionate, generous, loyal, sincere and bold Child of the King. These are just a few of the wonderful godly traits that can be found in Tesha. Watching her go through this journey of writing this book, it's awakened all these identity traits in her and more.

According to 2 Corinthians 5:17 (NLT), *"This means that anyone who belongs to Christ has become a new person. The old life is gone; a new life has begun!"* Eyes Wide Open will provide you with a pathway to your true identity in Christ. God has called us to be bold and courageous as we go out to tell the Good News of the Gospel. Knowing your identity will allow you to soar in kingdom building.

Eagle Wanda Finley

Edison, New Jersey

# ENDNOTES

1       Ostis B. Wilson, Jr., "The Sanctified Experience," *Timeless Truths*, https://library.timelesstruths.org/texts/Truths_on_Sanctification/The_Sanctified_Experience/

2       "51 Essential Bible Verses for Sanctification," *Bible Lyfe*, https://www.biblelyfe.com/blog/bible-verses-about-sanctification

3       David Oyedepo, "Vital Keys to a Sanctified Life!" *Vanguard*, https://www.vanguardngr.com/2012/02/vital-keys-to-a-sanctified-life

4       Oyedopo, "Vital Keys."

5       Kurt Selles, "The Holy Spirit Sanctifies Us," *Today Daily Devotional*, June 18, 2016, https://todaydevotional.com/devotions/the-holy-spirit-sanctifies-us

6       Karen Holmes, "'Be Still Doesn't Mean What You Think It Does..." *Inspired to Faith*, March 15, 2019, https://www.inspiredtofaith.com/2019/03/15/be-still-doesnt-mean-what-you-think-it-does/

7       "Mandate," *Encyclopedia.com*, https://www.encyclopedia.com/social-sciences-and-law/law/law/mandate

Made in the USA
Middletown, DE
11 February 2023

23770690R00050